Main

U.S.A. TRAVEL GUIDES

MONTANA

BY ANN HEINRICHS • ILLUSTRATED BY MATT KANIA

The Child's World®
childsworld.com

Published by The Child's World®
1980 Lookout Drive • Mankato, MN 56003-1705
800-599-READ • www.childsworld.com

Photo Credits
Photographs ©: Shutterstock Images, cover, 1, 20, 37
(top), 37 (bottom); National Park Service, 7; Brett Billings/
U.S. Fish and Wildlife Service, 8, 28; Lewis Kendall/
Bozeman Daily Chronicle/AP Images, 11; Adam Sings in
the Timber/Great Falls Tribune/AP Images, 12; Bureau of
Land Management, 15; Ernie Hathaway CC2.0, 16; Brian
Vikander Stock Connection USA/Newscom, 19; Radoslaw
Lecyk/Shutterstock Images, 23; SheltieBoy CC2.0, 24;
Tracy Elizabeth CC2.0, 27; Xavier Arnau/iStockphoto, 31;
iStockphoto, 32; Sarah Jessup/Shutterstock Images, 35

ISBN 9781503819665
LCCN 2016961179

Printing
Printed in the United States of America
PA02334

Ann Heinrichs is the author of more than 100 books for children and young adults. She has also enjoyed successful careers as a children's book editor and an advertising copywriter. Ann grew up in Fort Smith, Arkansas, and lives in Chicago, Illinois.

About the Author
Ann Heinrichs

Matt Kania loves maps and, as a kid, dreamed of making them. In school he studied geography and cartography, and today he makes maps for a living. Matt's favorite thing about drawing maps is learning about the places they represent. Many of the maps he has created can be found in books, magazines, videos, Web sites, and public places.

About the Map Illustrator
Matt Kania

On the cover: Going-to-the-Sun Road is a popular highway in Glacier National Park.

OUR MONTANA TRIP

Are you ready to explore Montana? You'll have the adventure of a lifetime there!

You'll round up cattle across the range. You'll pan for gold. You'll hang out with **wilderness** explorers. You'll climb mountains and meet wild animals. You'll learn about smoke jumping. And you'll dig for dinosaur bones!

That's just a taste of what's to come. So let's head on out. Just saddle up or buckle yourself in. We're off to see Montana!

WELCOME TO MONTANA

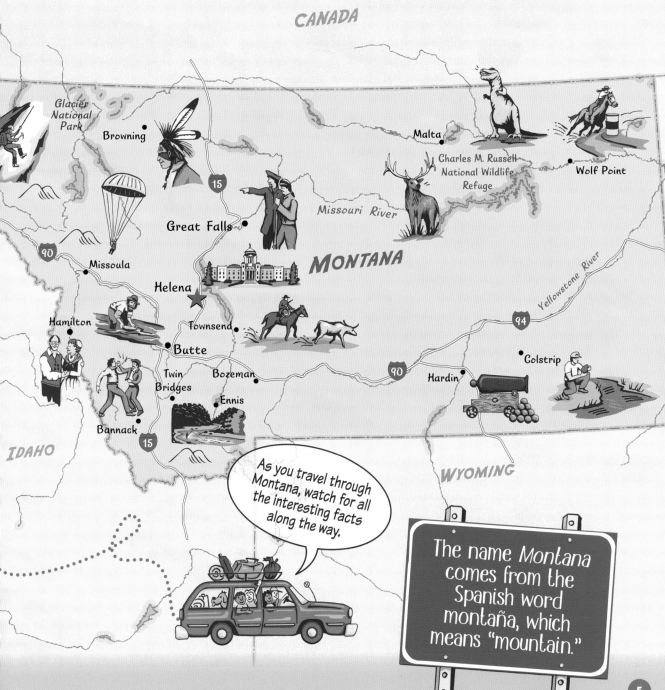

CANADA

Glacier National Park

Browning

Malta

Charles M. Russell National Wildlife Refuge

Wolf Point

15

Great Falls

Missouri River

90

Missoula

MONTANA

Helena

Yellowstone River

Hamilton

94

Townsend

Colstrip

Butte

Twin Bridges

Bozeman

90

Hardin

Ennis

Bannack

15

IDAHO

WYOMING

As you travel through Montana, watch for all the interesting facts along the way.

The name *Montana* comes from the Spanish word *montaña*, which means "mountain."

5

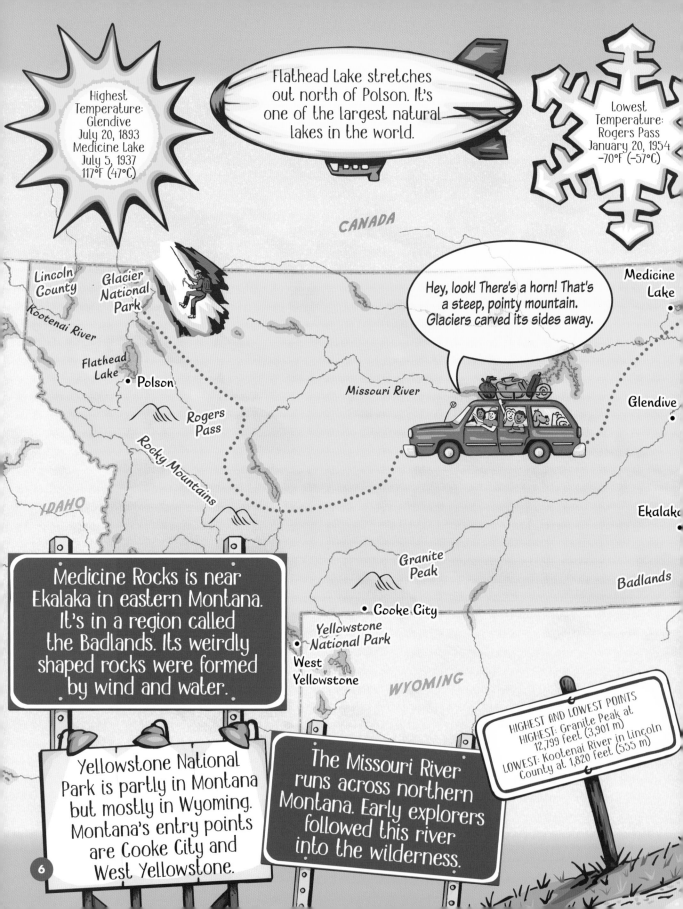

Highest
Temperature:
Glendive
July 20, 1893
Medicine Lake
July 5, 1937
117°F (47°C)

Flathead Lake stretches out north of Polson. It's one of the largest natural lakes in the world.

Lowest
Temperature:
Rogers Pass
January 20, 1954
−70°F (−57°C)

CANADA

Lincoln County

Glacier National Park

Kootenai River

Flathead Lake

Polson

Rogers Pass

Rocky Mountains

IDAHO

Missouri River

Hey, look! There's a horn! That's a steep, pointy mountain. Glaciers carved its sides away.

Medicine Lake

Glendive

Ekalaka

Granite Peak

Badlands

Cooke City

Yellowstone National Park

West Yellowstone

WYOMING

Medicine Rocks is near Ekalaka in eastern Montana. It's in a region called the Badlands. Its weirdly shaped rocks were formed by wind and water.

Yellowstone National Park is partly in Montana but mostly in Wyoming. Montana's entry points are Cooke City and West Yellowstone.

The Missouri River runs across northern Montana. Early explorers followed this river into the wilderness.

HIGHEST AND LOWEST POINTS
HIGHEST: Granite Peak at 12,799 feet (3,901 m)
LOWEST: Kootenai River in Lincoln County at 1,820 feet (555 m)

GLACIER NATIONAL PARK

Do you like rugged adventures? Then you'll love Glacier National Park. It's a challenge for mountain climbers. There are more than 100 mountains to explore.

Dozens of glaciers cling to the mountainsides. Glaciers are masses of snow and ice. They slide down the slopes very slowly.

This park covers a section of the Rocky Mountains. The Rockies rise in western Montana. Their snowcapped peaks glisten in the sunlight. Many rivers cut wide valleys through the mountains. Rolling plains cover eastern Montana. Here the sky looks really big. That's why Montana is called Big Sky Country!

Many beautiful lakes can be found in Glacier National Park.

THE CHARLES M. RUSSELL NATIONAL WILDLIFE REFUGE

Huge elk bellow their calls. Big, woolly mountain goats look down from above. Coyotes and foxes slink through the brush. Pelicans waddle around the lakeshore.

You're exploring the Charles M. Russell National Wildlife Refuge. It runs alongside Fort Peck Lake. Do you like big animals or tiny ones? You'll find them all here!

Glacier National Park is another great wildlife site. It has black bears, grizzly bears, and moose. Bighorn sheep paw at mountainside mosses. And graceful eagles sail through the Big Sky!

A herd of elk grazes in the Charles M. Russell National Wildlife Refuge.

STATE TREE:
PONDEROSA PINE

STATE FLOWER:
BITTERROOT

STATE BIRD:
WESTERN MEADOWLARK

The National Bison Range is near Moiese. It has herds of bison, or buffalo. Elk, deer, and antelope live there, too.

CANADA

Glacier National Park

Is that a chicken clucking? No, it's a sage grouse! Grouse make bubbling and cackling sounds.

Charles M. Russell National Wildlife Refuge

Fort Peck

Fort Peck Lake

• Moiese

Rare black-footed ferrets were reintroduced into the Charles M. Russell National Wildlife Refuge in 1994.

IDAHO

Red Lodge

Grasshopper Glacier is near Cooke City. There you can see grasshoppers that were trapped in the glacier long ago.

Cooke City

The National Park Service has ten sites in Montana.

West Yellowstone

WYOMING

Want to see grizzly bears and gray wolves up close? Visit the Grizzly and Wolf Discovery Center near West Yellowstone.

The Yellowstone Wildlife Sanctuary is in Red Lodge. It keeps wild animals that can't return to the wild. Many have been injured. You can pet some of them!

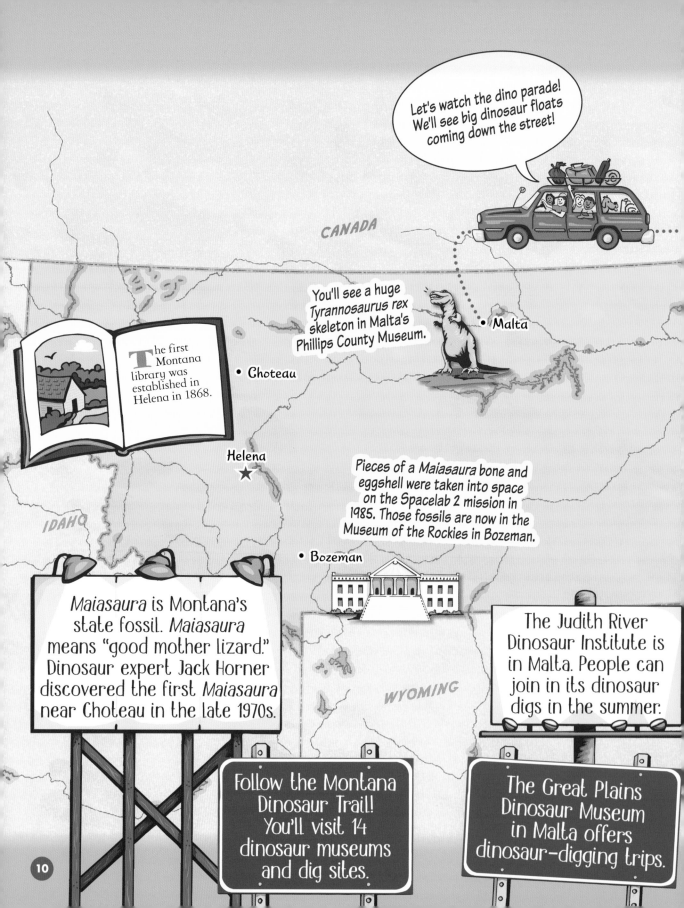

Let's watch the dino parade! We'll see big dinosaur floats coming down the street!

CANADA

You'll see a huge *Tyrannosaurus rex* skeleton in Malta's Phillips County Museum.

• Malta

The first Montana library was established in Helena in 1868.

• Choteau

Helena ★

Pieces of a Maiasaura bone and eggshell were taken into space on the Spacelab 2 mission in 1985. Those fossils are now in the Museum of the Rockies in Bozeman.

IDAHO

• Bozeman

Maiasaura is Montana's state fossil. *Maiasaura* means "good mother lizard." Dinosaur expert Jack Horner discovered the first *Maiasaura* near Choteau in the late 1970s.

WYOMING

The Judith River Dinosaur Institute is in Malta. People can join in its dinosaur digs in the summer.

Follow the Montana Dinosaur Trail! You'll visit 14 dinosaur museums and dig sites.

The Great Plains Dinosaur Museum in Malta offers dinosaur-digging trips.

10

MALTA'S DINOSAUR FESTIVAL

Would you like onions on your bronto burger? Don't worry. It's not really made of *Brontosaurus* meat. But it's a perfect snack for today's event. You're at the Montana Dinosaur Festival in Malta!

This festival celebrates some old Montana residents— dinosaurs! You'll dig for bones in a dino pit. You'll learn to make **fossil** molds. And you'll chat with scientists who dig for dinosaurs.

Montana's a great state for dinosaur digging. Many kinds of dinosaurs once roamed here. One was *Triceratops*, with three pointy horns. Another was the fearsome *Tyrannosaurus rex*. Good thing it's not around anymore. It could have swallowed a human whole!

Dinosaur expert Jack Horner talks to museum visitors in Bozeman.

NORTH AMERICAN INDIAN DAYS

Children and grown-ups perform ceremonial dances. Tall white tepees surround the camp. This is North American Indian Days! It's in Browning on the Blackfeet Indian **Reservation**.

Native Americans from around the country attend this festival. Montana's Blackfeet Native Americans are the **hosts**. The Blackfeet are among Montana's Plains Native Americans. They once hunted buffalo across the eastern plains. They made clothes and tepees from buffalo hides.

Other groups made their homes in the Rockies. They gathered plants in the forests. They hunted and caught fish. They made tools from wood, bones, and rocks.

More than 60,000 Native Americans live in Montana today. There are seven reservations and 12 Native American tribes in Montana.

A Native American girl sings at North American Indian Days in Browning.

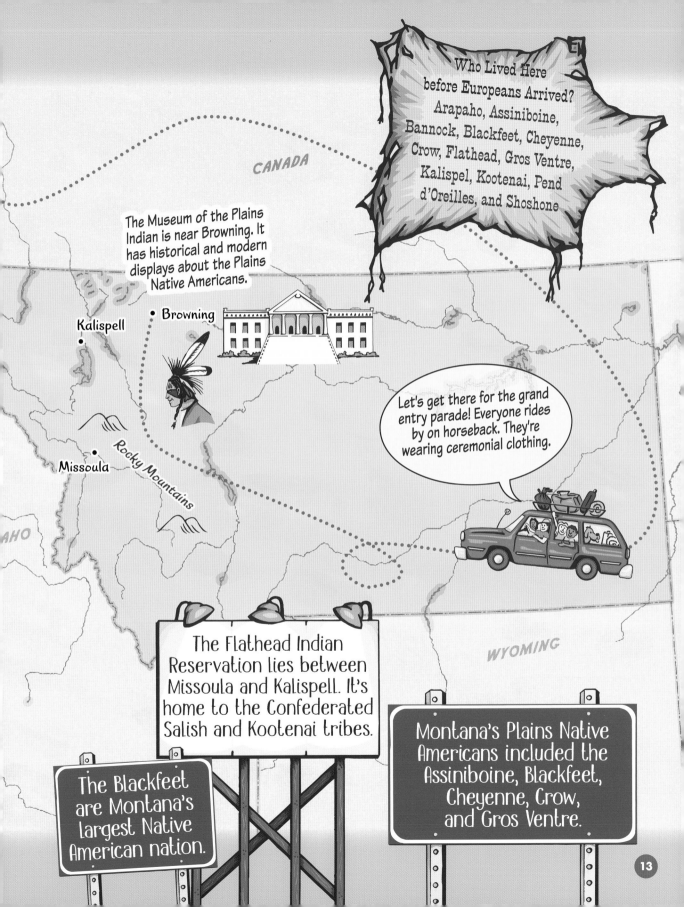

Who Lived Here before Europeans Arrived? Arapaho, Assiniboine, Bannock, Blackfeet, Cheyenne, Crow, Flathead, Gros Ventre, Kalispel, Kootenai, Pend d'Oreilles, and Shoshone

CANADA

The Museum of the Plains Indian is near Browning. It has historical and modern displays about the Plains Native Americans.

Kalispell

Browning

Missoula

Rocky Mountains

Let's get there for the grand entry parade! Everyone rides by on horseback. They're wearing ceremonial clothing.

WYOMING

AHO

The Flathead Indian Reservation lies between Missoula and Kalispell. It's home to the Confederated Salish and Kootenai tribes.

Montana's Plains Native Americans included the Assiniboine, Blackfeet, Cheyenne, Crow, and Gros Ventre.

The Blackfeet are Montana's largest Native American nation.

13

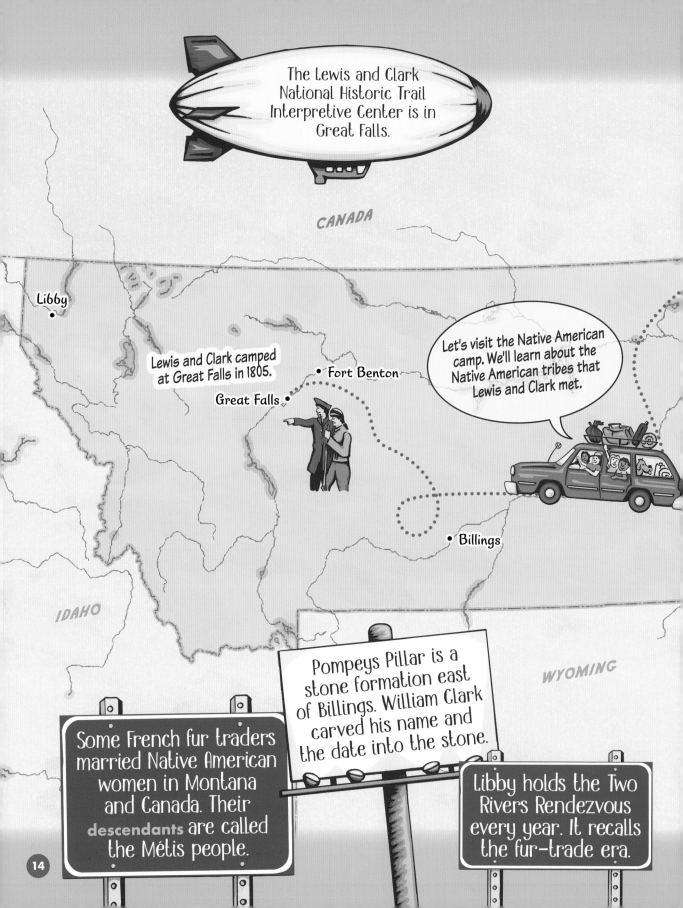

The Lewis and Clark National Historic Trail Interpretive Center is in Great Falls.

CANADA

Libby

Lewis and Clark camped at Great Falls in 1805.

Fort Benton

Great Falls

Let's visit the Native American camp. We'll learn about the Native American tribes that Lewis and Clark met.

Billings

IDAHO

WYOMING

Pompeys Pillar is a stone formation east of Billings. William Clark carved his name and the date into the stone.

Some French fur traders married Native American women in Montana and Canada. Their **descendants** are called the Métis people.

Libby holds the Two Rivers Rendezvous every year. It recalls the fur-trade era.

THE LEWIS AND CLARK FESTIVAL IN GREAT FALLS

Mmm—smell those campfires. And what's cooking? Some nice, juicy *boudin blanc*! That's a type of sausage. Chat with people around the camp. They'll show you how explorers worked and lived. It's the Lewis and Clark Festival in Great Falls!

Explorers Meriwether Lewis and William Clark crossed Montana. They were trying to reach the Pacific Ocean. They passed through in 1805 and 1806. Their wilderness journey was tiring and dangerous.

After that, fur trappers and traders arrived. Many of the trappers were Frenchmen from Canada. One fur company built Fort Benton in 1847. That's now Montana's oldest town.

Check out Pompeys Pillar near Billings to learn more about Lewis and Clark's journey through Montana.

WILD TIMES IN BANNACK

Ride a stagecoach through town. Chat with miners in their tent camp. Learn about some of Montana's most famous outlaws. It's time for Bannack Days! This event celebrates Bannack's colorful past.

Gold was discovered in Montana in 1862. Mining towns sprang up overnight. They included Bannack, Diamond City, and Virginia City. Outlaws roamed through the mining camps. They often robbed miners.

Meanwhile, ranchers began raising cattle in Montana. Railroads reached Montana in 1881. Then ranchers could ship cattle to faraway markets.

Visit the ghost town of Bannack to learn more about Montana's gold mining history.

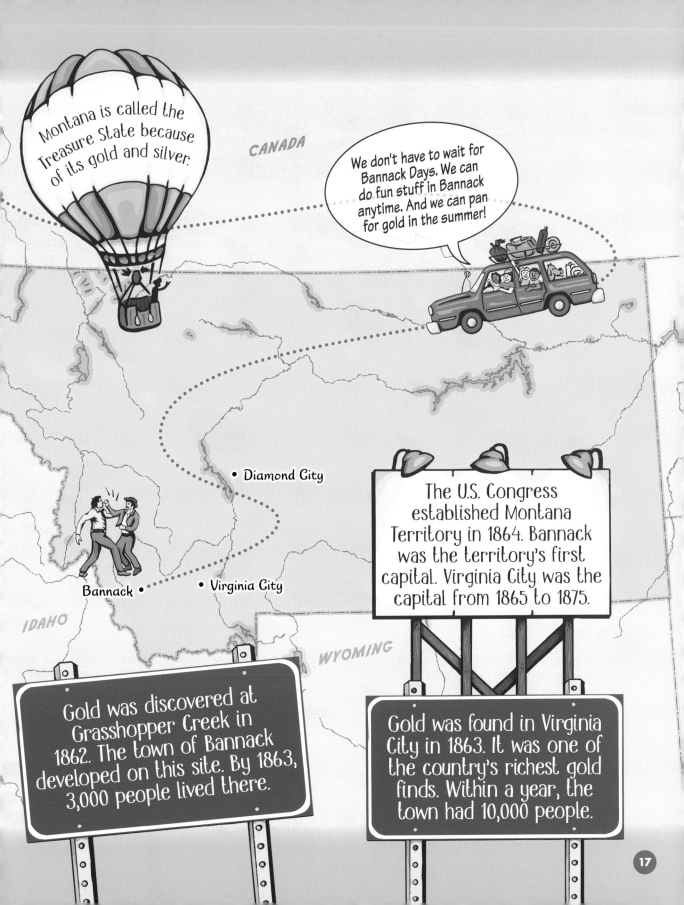

Montana is called the Treasure State because of its gold and silver.

CANADA

We don't have to wait for Bannack Days. We can do fun stuff in Bannack anytime. And we can pan for gold in the summer!

• Diamond City

• Virginia City

Bannack •

IDAHO

WYOMING

The U.S. Congress established Montana Territory in 1864. Bannack was the territory's first capital. Virginia City was the capital from 1865 to 1875.

Gold was discovered at Grasshopper Creek in 1862. The town of Bannack developed on this site. By 1863, 3,000 people lived there.

Gold was found in Virginia City in 1863. It was one of the country's richest gold finds. Within a year, the town had 10,000 people.

Moving cattle is hard work! But we can relax at night. We'll listen to cowboy poetry and sing campfire songs!

Whitefish holds Huckleberry Days every year. Its events include a huckleberry pie-eating contest. Huckleberries are little purple fruits that grow on a bush.

CANADA

Whitefish •

The state fair takes place in Great Falls in late July each year.

Choteau •

Great Falls •

Townsend •

Reed Point •

IDAHO

WYOMING

Reed Point holds the Great Mountain Sheep Drive every year. Hundreds of sheep go running down the town's main street.

Choteau holds the Threshing Bee every year. Threshing is separating the grain from crops such as wheat or hay.

What Does Montana Raise? Beef cattle, wheat, hay, barley, and milk

THE MONTANA HIGH COUNTRY CATTLE DRIVE

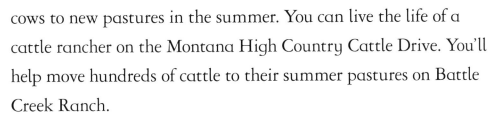

Gallop across the range chasing cattle. Sleep under the stars as a coyote howls. You're taking part in the Montana High Country Cattle Drive in Townsend.

Cattle ranchers in Montana move herds of cows to new pastures in the summer. You can live the life of a cattle rancher on the Montana High Country Cattle Drive. You'll help move hundreds of cattle to their summer pastures on Battle Creek Ranch.

Farms and ranches cover more than half of Montana. Beef cattle are the top farm product. Huge ranches stretch out across the plains. Some ranchers raise dairy cattle and sheep. Many farmers grow crops. Montana's top crop is wheat.

Montana ranchers drive cattle to winter and summer pastures each year.

LITTLE BIG HORN DAYS NEAR HARDIN

Native Americans and soldiers are locked in battle. Their cries rise amid smoke and dust. It seems like a movie. But you're right there. It's the Battle of the Little Bighorn. People act out this battle near Hardin every year during Little Big Horn Days.

Gold was found near this area. The U.S. government wanted the Native Americans out. Army officer George Custer was sent there in 1876. He was to move the Native Americans to reservations.

Custer's force attacked a group of Sioux, Arapaho, and Cheyenne Native Americans. The Native Americans defeated Custer and his men. But the U.S. Army gathered other troops. Within five years, most of the Native Americans had been defeated. They were forced onto reservations in present-day South Dakota.

Men reenact the Battle of Little Bighorn during Montana's Little Bighorn Days.

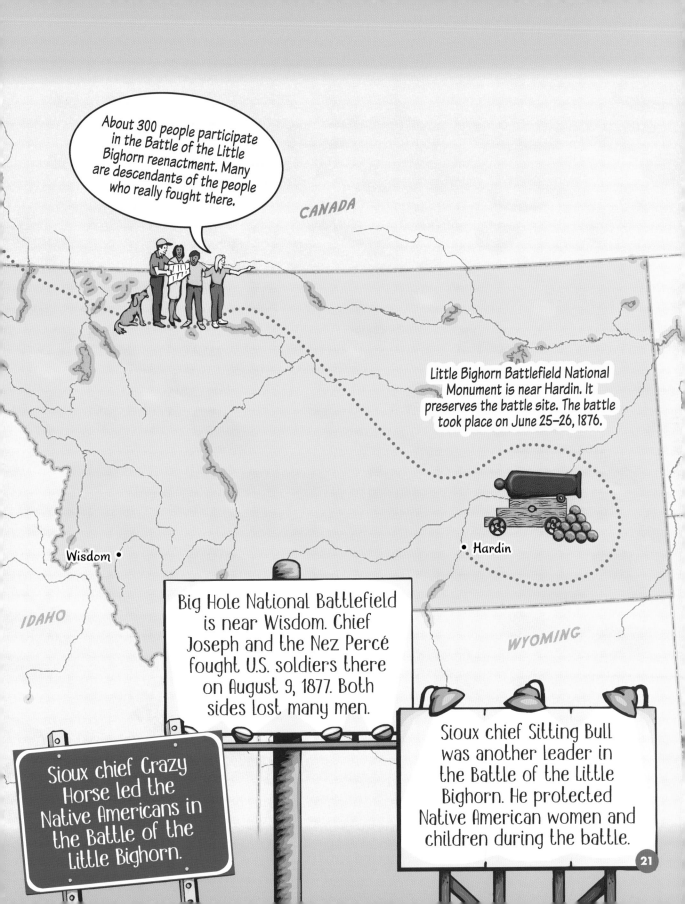

About 300 people participate in the Battle of the Little Bighorn reenactment. Many are descendants of the people who really fought there.

CANADA

Little Bighorn Battlefield National Monument is near Hardin. It preserves the battle site. The battle took place on June 25–26, 1876.

Wisdom •

• Hardin

IDAHO

WYOMING

Big Hole National Battlefield is near Wisdom. Chief Joseph and the Nez Percé fought U.S. soldiers there on August 9, 1877. Both sides lost many men.

Sioux chief Crazy Horse led the Native Americans in the Battle of the Little Bighorn.

Sioux chief Sitting Bull was another leader in the Battle of the Little Bighorn. He protected Native American women and children during the battle.

21

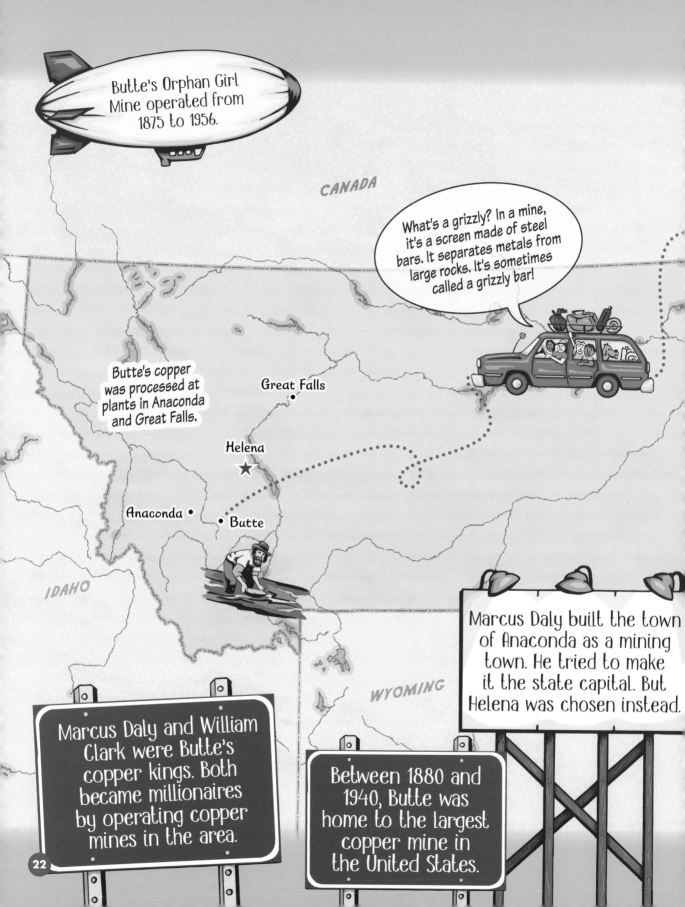

Butte's Orphan Girl Mine operated from 1875 to 1956.

CANADA

What's a grizzly? In a mine, it's a screen made of steel bars. It separates metals from large rocks. It's sometimes called a grizzly bar!

Butte's copper was processed at plants in Anaconda and Great Falls.

Great Falls

Helena ★

Anaconda • • Butte

IDAHO

WYOMING

Marcus Daly built the town of Anaconda as a mining town. He tried to make it the state capital. But Helena was chosen instead.

Marcus Daly and William Clark were Butte's copper kings. Both became millionaires by operating copper mines in the area.

Between 1880 and 1940, Butte was home to the largest copper mine in the United States.

BUTTE'S WORLD MUSEUM OF MINING

Take a tour of the Orphan Girl Mine. See the mine shaft that went deep underground. People and mules traveled down in a cage. Then tour Hell Roarin' Gulch. It's built like an 1890s mining town. You can even try panning for gold. You're exploring Butte's World Museum of Mining!

Gold mining began in Butte in 1864. Then silver was discovered in the area in 1875. Next, copper was discovered in Butte Hill. The town of Butte is on the south-facing slope of this hill. Soon it was called the Richest Hill on Earth. The Anaconda Mining Company operated dozens of mines. **Immigrants** from many countries came to work there.

Explore an 1800s-era mining town at Butte's World Museum of Mining.

THE BITTERROOT CELTIC GAMES IN HAMILTON

Listen to bagpipe music. Watch traditional Irish and Scottish dances. You're at the Bitterroot Celtic Games in Hamilton!

Copper king Marcus Daly founded the town of Hamilton in 1894. Daly was an Irish immigrant. He built sawmills in Bitterroot Valley. Many Scottish, Irish, and Welsh immigrants worked in his mills and mines. The Bitterroot Celtic Games celebrates Hamilton's Irish and Scottish **heritage**.

Many immigrants settled in Montana in the 1800s and early 1900s. Some people came from Germany, Italy, Finland, or Norway. Not everyone worked in mines. Many settlers kept farms and ranches. People came from eastern Europe and China, too. It's great to enjoy their **customs** at festivals!

Listen to some traditional bagpipe music at the Bitterroot Celtic Games.

Montana's state motto is "oro y plata." This is Latin for "gold and silver."

Wait! I'm mixed up! How many William Clarks did Montana have? Two: the explorer and the copper king.

CANADA

Montana had lots of millionaires in the 1880s. They got rich from gold mining.

• Missoula

★
Helena

Anaconda •

IDAHO

Copper king William Clark wanted Helena to be the state capital. He won out over Marcus Daly, who favored Anaconda.

Gold was discovered in Last Chance Gulch in 1864. That stretch of land became Helena's main street. What's the street's name today? Last Chance Gulch!

Montana was the 41st state to enter the Union. It joined on November 8, 1889.

WYOMING

Jeannette Rankin was born in Missoula. In 1916, she became the first woman elected to the U.S. House of Representatives.

In the capitol is a giant painting by famous Montana artist Charles M. Russell. It's called *Lewis and Clark Meeting Indians at Ross' Hole.*

THE STATE CAPITOL IN HELENA

See that shiny dome on top of the capitol? Guess what it's made of? Copper, of course! Copper played a big part in Montana's history. No wonder it tops the state government building in Helena.

Montana's government is divided into three branches. One branch makes the laws. Its members meet in the capitol. Another branch carries out the laws. The governor heads this branch. Judges make up the third branch. They listen to cases in courts. Then they decide whether laws have been broken.

The Helena state capitol building opened in 1902.

Welcome to Helena, the capital of Montana!

CLEANING UP IN COLSTRIP

Most mining goes on underground. But sometimes valuable minerals lie near the surface. Miners scoop out the land to get them.

Surface mining began in Colstrip in the 1920s. The pits and dirt piles became a terrible mess. In the 1970s, Colstrip began to clean up. Its mines began massive reclamation projects. Reclamation involves repairing damaged land.

Colstrip now has 32 public parks and 7 miles (11.3 km) of walking trails. You'll find some grassy lands and clean, sparkling streams. One area was once a home for sharp-tailed grouse. The males do a dance to attract females. Now some of their dancing ground is back again.

Sharp-tailed grouse live in grassland areas, including parts of Colstrip.

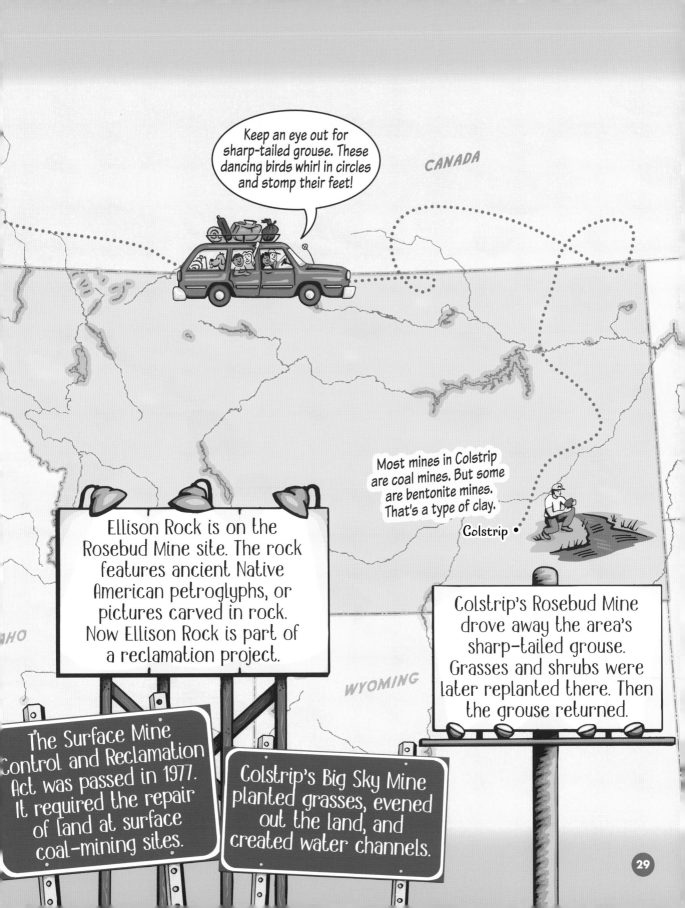

Keep an eye out for sharp-tailed grouse. These dancing birds whirl in circles and stomp their feet!

CANADA

Most mines in Colstrip are coal mines. But some are bentonite mines. That's a type of clay.

Colstrip •

Ellison Rock is on the Rosebud Mine site. The rock features ancient Native American petroglyphs, or pictures carved in rock. Now Ellison Rock is part of a reclamation project.

Colstrip's Rosebud Mine drove away the area's sharp-tailed grouse. Grasses and shrubs were later replanted there. Then the grouse returned.

WYOMING

AHO

The Surface Mine Control and Reclamation Act was passed in 1977. It required the repair of land at surface coal-mining sites.

Colstrip's Big Sky Mine planted grasses, evened out the land, and created water channels.

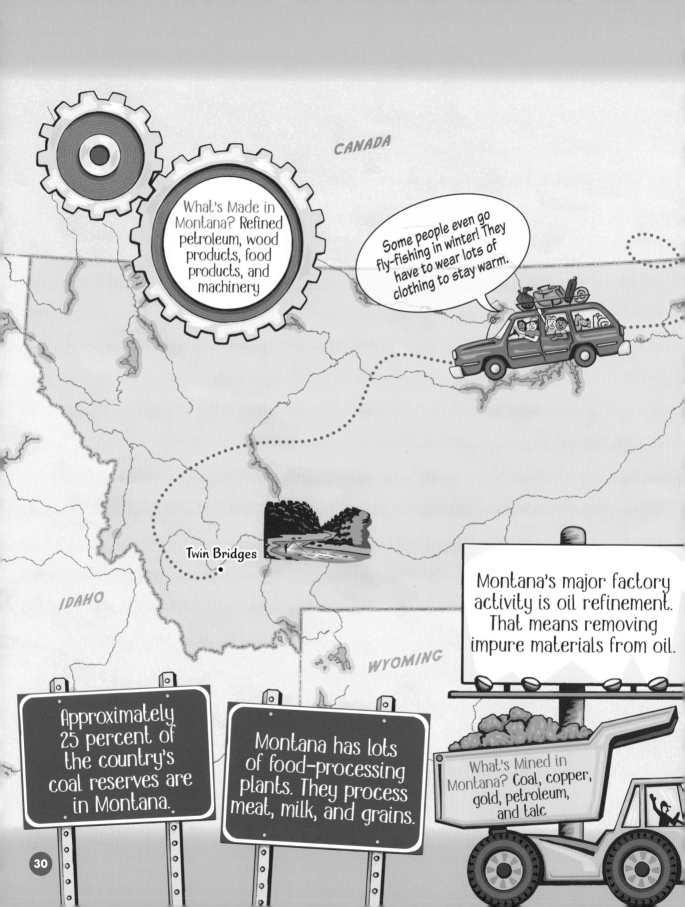

CANADA

What's Made in Montana? Refined petroleum, wood products, food products, and machinery

Some people even go fly-fishing in winter! They have to wear lots of clothing to stay warm.

Twin Bridges

IDAHO

WYOMING

Montana's major factory activity is oil refinement. That means removing impure materials from oil.

Approximately 25 percent of the country's coal reserves are in Montana.

Montana has lots of food-processing plants. They process meat, milk, and grains.

What's Mined in Montana? Coal, copper, gold, petroleum, and talc

FLY-FISHING IN TWIN BRIDGES

S wish! You flick your wrist and cast your line. It arcs into the middle of the river. You reel your line in quickly, hoping to catch a fish. You are fly-fishing in Twin Bridges.

Fly-fishing is popular in Montana. It is similar to regular fishing, also known as spin fishing. But the pole is lighter. Fly-fishing is often done in rivers while spin fishing is often done in lakes.

Tour R.L. Winston Rod Company in Twin Bridges to find out how fly-fishing rods are made. A lot of time and care go into making fly-fishing rods. The R.L. Winston Rod Company has been making fly-fishing rods for more than 80 years.

Fly-fishing is a popular sport in Montana.

WOLF POINT'S WILD HORSE STAMPEDE

Wild horses run madly around the ring. Three cowboys chase them on foot. They hope to catch a horse and saddle it. Then they'll try to ride it. You're watching the Wild Horse Stampede in Wolf Point!

This is Montana's oldest rodeo. It features many other riding and roping events. Many Montana towns host rodeos. Cowboys and cowgirls show off their skills there.

Montana's a great place for outdoor adventures, too. People love camping, hiking, and mountain climbing. Boaters and fishers enjoy the lakes and streams. In the winter, people go snowmobiling and skiing. Everyone likes to gaze at the Big Sky!

The excitement never ends at a Montana rodeo!

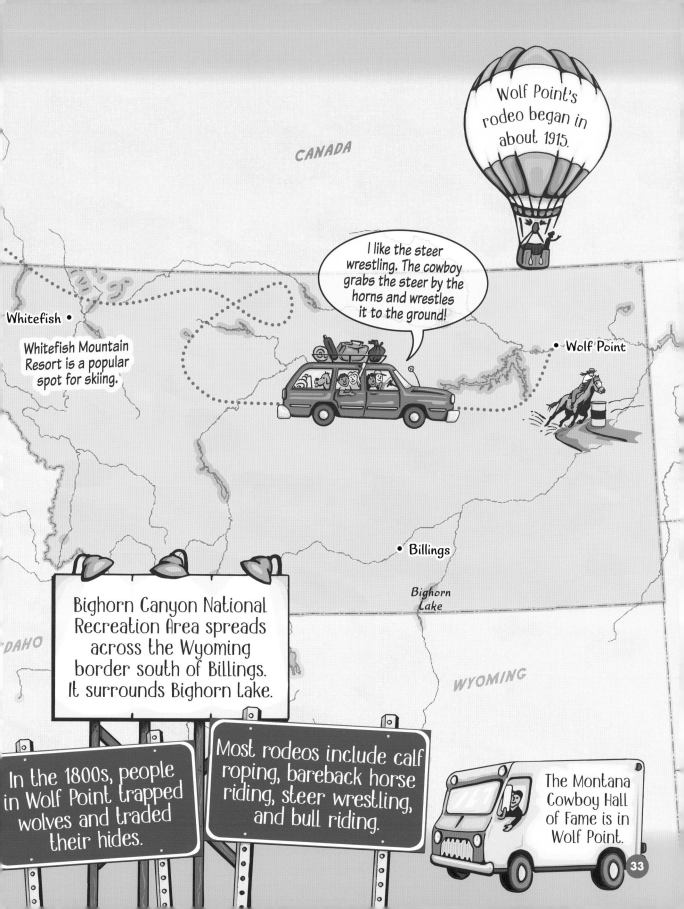

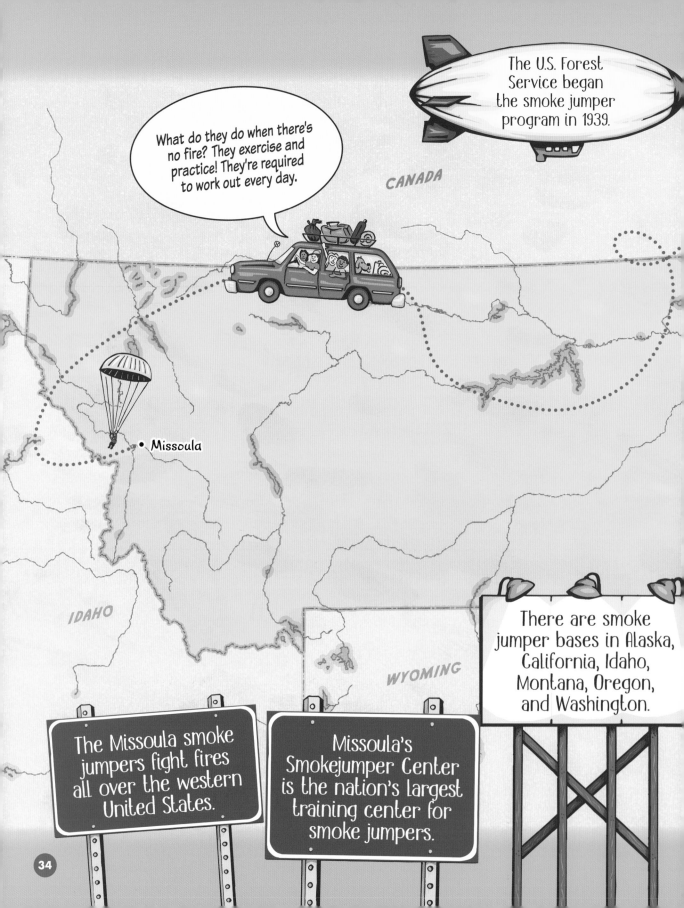

What do they do when there's no fire? They exercise and practice! They're required to work out every day.

The U.S. Forest Service began the smoke jumper program in 1939.

CANADA

Missoula

IDAHO

WYOMING

There are smoke jumper bases in Alaska, California, Idaho, Montana, Oregon, and Washington.

The Missoula smoke jumpers fight fires all over the western United States.

Missoula's Smokejumper Center is the nation's largest training center for smoke jumpers.

SMOKE JUMPING IN MISSOULA

Would you like to be a firefighter? Would you like to fight forest fires? How about parachuting out of an airplane? Some people do all these things at once. They're called smoke jumpers!

Just drop by Missoula's Smokejumper Visitor Center. You'll learn how smoke jumpers train and work. You'll see the **loft** where they practice jumps.

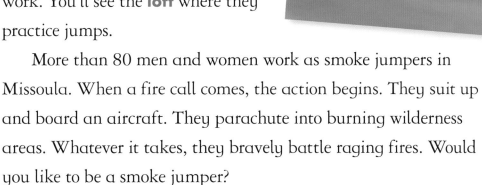

More than 80 men and women work as smoke jumpers in Missoula. When a fire call comes, the action begins. They suit up and board an aircraft. They parachute into burning wilderness areas. Whatever it takes, they bravely battle raging fires. Would you like to be a smoke jumper?

A smoke jumper parachutes through the sky above Missoula.

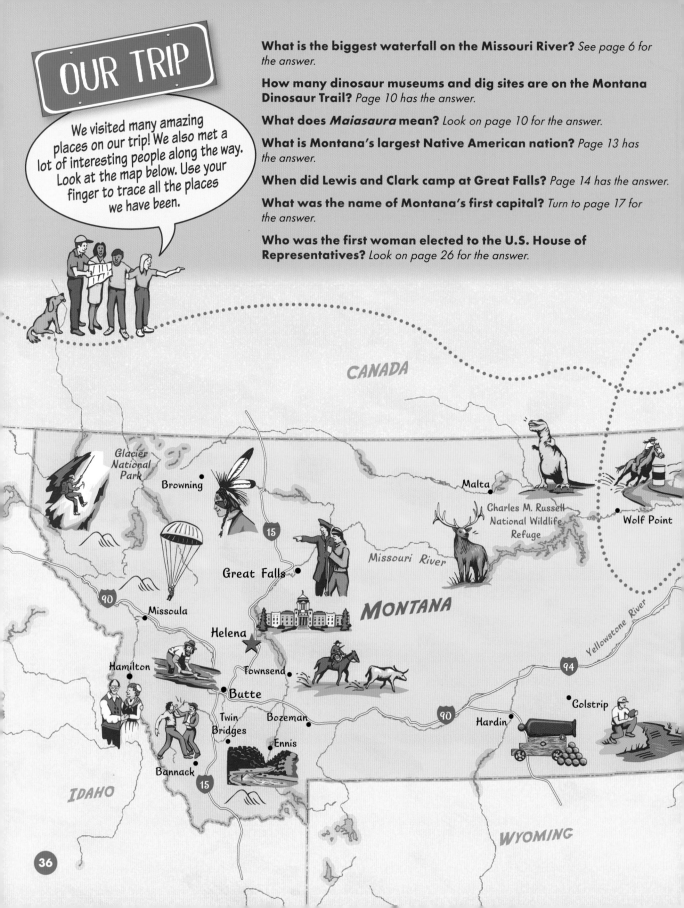

OUR TRIP

We visited many amazing places on our trip! We also met a lot of interesting people along the way. Look at the map below. Use your finger to trace all the places we have been.

What is the biggest waterfall on the Missouri River? *See page 6 for the answer.*

How many dinosaur museums and dig sites are on the Montana Dinosaur Trail? *Page 10 has the answer.*

What does *Maiasaura* mean? *Look on page 10 for the answer.*

What is Montana's largest Native American nation? *Page 13 has the answer.*

When did Lewis and Clark camp at Great Falls? *Page 14 has the answer.*

What was the name of Montana's first capital? *Turn to page 17 for the answer.*

Who was the first woman elected to the U.S. House of Representatives? *Look on page 26 for the answer.*

CANADA

Glacier National Park
Browning
Malta
Charles M. Russell National Wildlife Refuge
Wolf Point
15
Great Falls
Missouri River
90
Missoula
MONTANA
Helena
Yellowstone River
Hamilton
Townsend
94
Butte
Twin Bridges
Bozeman
90
Hardin
Colstrip
Ennis
Bannack
15
IDAHO
WYOMING

STATE SYMBOLS

State animal: Grizzly bear

State bird: Western meadowlark

State butterfly: Mourning cloak

State fish: Blackspotted cutthroat trout

State flower: Bitterroot

State fossil: *Maiasaura* (duck-billed dinosaur)

State gemstones: Agate and sapphire

State grass: Bluebunch wheatgrass

State tree: Ponderosa pine

State seal

STATE SONG

"MONTANA"

*Words by Charles C. Cohan, music by
Joseph E. Howard*

Tell me of that Treasure State
Story always new,
Tell of its beauties grand
And its hearts so true.
Mountains of sunset fire
The land I love the best
Let me grasp the hand of one
From out the golden West.

Chorus:
Montana, Montana,
Glory of the West
Of all the states from coast to
coast,
You're easily the best.

Montana, Montana,
Where skies are always blue
M-O-N-T-A-N-A,
Montana, I love you.

Each country has its flow'r;
Each one plays a part,
Each bloom brings a longing
hope
To some lonely heart.
Bitterroot to me is dear
Growing in my land
Sing then that glorious air
The one I understand.

(Chorus)

That was a great trip! We have traveled all over Montana. There are a few places that we didn't have time for, though. Next time, we plan to check out the Spirit of the North Sled Dog Adventure in Ennis. A team of huskies pulls visitors over a mountain trail. The huskies are very friendly and love being out in the snow!

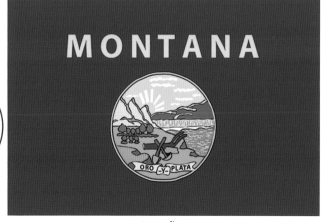

State flag

FAMOUS PEOPLE

Bergoust, Eric (1969–), skier and Olympic gold medalist

Borman, Frank (1928–), astronaut

Carvey, Dana (1955–), comedian

Cooper, Gary (1901–1961), actor

Horner, Jack (1946–), paleontologist

Jackson, Phil (1945–), basketball coach

Knievel, Evel (1938–2007), daredevil

Kramer, Jerry (1936–), football player

Loy, Myrna (1905–1993), actor

Maclean, Norman (1902–1990), author and teacher

Mansfield, Mike (1903–2001), politician

McNally, Dave (1942–2002), baseball player

Montgomery, George (1916–2000), actor

Paolini, Christopher (1983–), author

Patent, Dorothy Hinshaw (1940–), children's author

Plenty Coups (ca. 1848–1932), Native American chief of the Crow Nation

Rankin, Jeannette (1880–1973), politician

Russell, Charles Marion (1864–1926), painter

Swingley, Doug (1953–), Iditarod sled dog race champion

Washakie (ca. 1804–1900), Native American chief of the Shoshone Nation

Williams, Michelle (1980–), actor

WORDS TO KNOW

descendants (di-SEND-uhnts) someone's children, grandchildren, great-grandchildren, and so on

fossil (FOSS-uhl) a remain or print of an animal or plant that lived long ago

hosts (HOHSTS) people who open their homes or territory to guests

immigrants (IM-uh-gruhnts) people who leave their home country and move to another country

loft (LOFT) a platform high above the ground floor

reservation (rez-ur-VAY-shuhn) land set aside for a special purpose, such as for Native Americans

wilderness (WIL-dur-niss) a natural area that's rough and wild

TO LEARN MORE

IN THE LIBRARY

Oachs, Emily Rose. *Montana*. Minneapolis, MN: Bellwether Media, 2014.

Roxburgh, Ellis. *Sitting Bull vs. George Armstrong Custer: The Battle of the Little Bighorn*. New York, NY: Gareth Stevens, 2016.

Yasuda, Anita. *Native Nations of the Plains*. Mankato, MN: The Child's World, 2016.

ON THE WEB

Visit our Web site for links about Montana:

childsworld.com/links

Note to Parents, Teachers, and Librarians: We routinely verify our Web links to make sure they are safe and active sites. So encourage your readers to check them out!

PLACES TO VISIT OR CONTACT

Montana Historical Society

mhs.mt.gov
PO Box 201201
225 North Roberts
Helena, MT 59620
406/444-2694

For more information about the history of Montana

Montana Office of Tourism

visitmt.com
301 South Park Avenue
PO Box 200533
Helena, MT 59620
800/847-4868

For more information about traveling in Montana

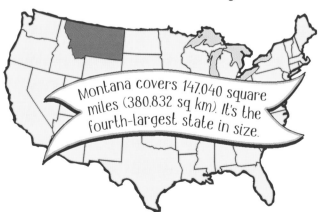

Montana covers 147,040 square miles (380,832 sq km). It's the fourth-largest state in size.

INDEX

Bye, Big Sky Country
We had a great time.
We'll come back soon!